READABOUT

Colour

© 1992 Franklin Watts

Franklin Watts
96 Leonard Street
London EC2A 4RH

Franklin Watts Australia
14 Mars Road
Lane Cove
NSW 2066

UK ISBN: 0 7496 0784 X

A CIP catalogue record for this book
is available from the British Library

Editor: Ambreen Husain
Design: K and Co

Printed in Hong Kong

READABOUT
Colour

Text: Henry Pluckrose
Photography: Chris Fairclough

Franklin Watts
London/New York/Sydney/Toronto

Our world is full
of colour.
There is colour in leaves
and in flowers,
colour in the feathers
of birds,
colour in the wings
of butterflies
and in the scales of fish.

There is colour in the sea
and colour in the sky.
There is colour
in shells, stones
and sand.

You cannot see colours
without light.
Light comes to us
from the sun.

The light from the sun
is made up of the colours
red, orange, yellow,
green, blue, indigo
and violet.
We call these colours
the spectrum.
You can see them
in a rainbow.

Our eyes 'read' the colours
we see.
When sunlight falls
onto these things
the red, orange, yellow
and green of the sun's light
are absorbed.
Blue light is reflected.
They all look blue.

These things absorb the orange, yellow, green and blue of the sun's light. They reflect red.

Each colour has many shades. These vegetables are all green...

and these clothes
are all yellow.
Is the cabbage
exactly the same colour
as the lettuce?

The colours we use
for painting
are made from pigments.
Some pigments are made
by grinding earth
into fine powder.
The powder is mixed
with oil or with water
to make paint.

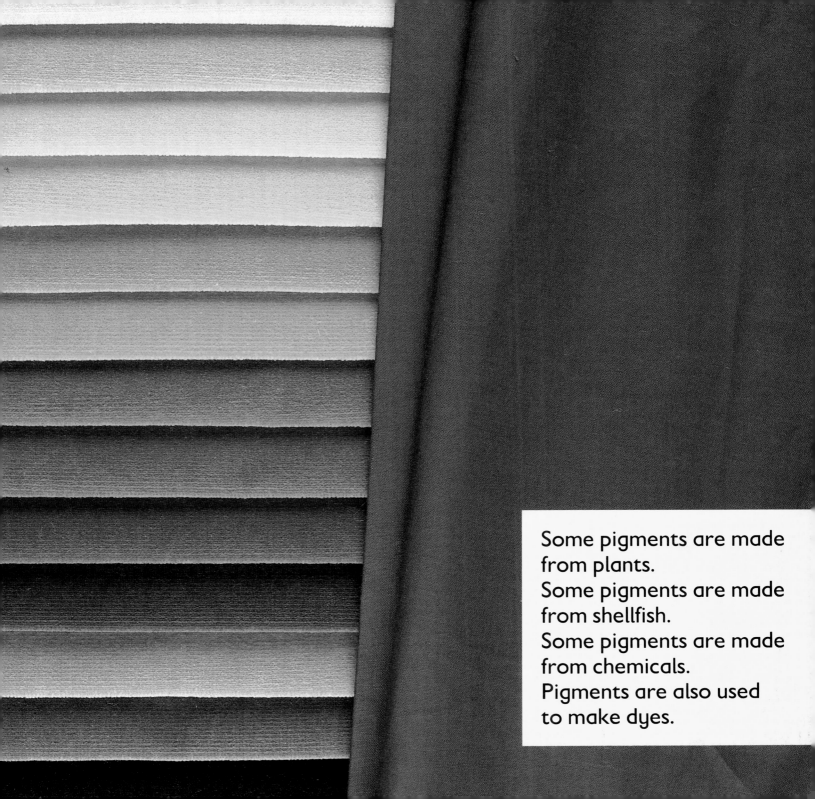

Some pigments are made
from plants.
Some pigments are made
from shellfish.
Some pigments are made
from chemicals.
Pigments are also used
to make dyes.

When you paint
or draw with crayons
or pastels
you are using pigments.
The most important
painting colours
are red, yellow and blue.

If you mix red and yellow
you make orange.
If you mix blue and yellow
you make green.
What happens when you mix
red and blue?

Red, orange and yellow
are called 'hot' colours.
Can you think why?

Green and blue
somehow help us to feel cool.
They are 'cold' colours.

We use colours
to give information
to drivers of trains
and cars.

Why do you think
the colour red
is used to warn of danger?

We use colours
in team games…

and supporters
wear colours too!

Some people wear clothes
of special colours,
for special occasions,
for religious reasons,
for their work...

or just for fun.

Animals, insects and birds
use colour
to give messages
about themselves.
The peacock uses
his brightly coloured tail
to attract a mate.

The coloured stripes of the bee give a warning. 'Don't touch me!'

Our skin, our eyes,
our hair
are also coloured.

It would be very boring
if everybody looked
just the same.

Can you imagine what life would be like without colours?